Duluth
Then & Now

PRESENTED BY THE DULUTH NEWS TRIBUNE

Published by Pediment Publishing, a division of The Pediment Group, Inc. www.pediment.com Printed in the U.S.A.

IKONICS

CORPORATION

*Bringing Unique Imaging Solutions
to the People of the World*

From its screen printing roots as ChromaGlo
in 1952, through decades of prosperity as
The Chromaline Corporation, and now, as
IKONICS, the character of the IKONICS Corporation
reflects the innovation, work ethic and community
spirit inherent to the Duluth area.

**4832 Grand Avenue, Duluth, MN 55807
phone: 218-628-2217 | fax: 218-628-3245
www.ikonics.com | info@ikonics.com**

FOREWORD

The years that shaped Duluth, and then reshaped it, from a wilderness outpost to a major Great Lakes port, could fill volumes.

And do.

Some years jump out.

There was 1855 when Henry Wheeler used brownstone quarried from what is now Duluth's Fond du Lac neighborhood to build a steam sawmill. About 15 years later, commercial production of the red-dawn sandstone began, giving Duluth a warm charm and the roots of an old-world look and feel it still boasts today. The best example is Old Central, which opened as a high school in 1892. The castle of a structure is now the school district's administration building.

There was 1869 when only 14 families celebrated New Year's Day in Duluth. By the Fourth of July, more than 3,500 people were here with more on the way. Many of them arrived on a new railroad financier Jay Cooke helped to bring from St. Paul. A boomtown that year, Duluth saw grand houses fill its hillside and its first newspaper begin publication. A telegraph linked Duluth to the outside world for the first time.

1905 is the year Duluth's landmark aerial bridge was built. The first of its kind in the United States and among only five of its style in the world, the original Aerial Ferry Bridge featured a gondola hung from a superstructure that passed over the Duluth ship canal. Today's famous rising road deck replaced the gondola in 1930.

In 1909, the county courthouse opened, the first of four buildings that make up the Duluth Civic Center Mall. Designed by noted American architect Daniel Burnham, the mall is one of Minnesota's best examples of the City Beautiful Movement of the early 1900s.

Finally, there's 1972, the year U.S. Steel announced it would end steel production at Duluth Works. Thousands of people lost jobs and a once-proud Duluth fell on some of its darkest days. Houses were abandoned and torn down. Once-grand structures were allowed to fall into disrepair.

But the city rebounded, beginning in about the 1980s. Old buildings were replaced. Canal Park was reinvented as the heart of an emerging tourism industry. Other industries emerged, including health care and higher education. Bricked streets filled downtown. Skywalks connected buildings.

Duluth changed.

Yet again.

Gone are the famous incline railway, the nation's largest curling club, the fur posts, Park Point's spectacular boat club, many of the grand theaters of the early 1900s and more.

But Old Central is still here. And the Civic Center and the Glensheen mansion and the old armory and Enger Tower and Skyline Parkway. And the big blue lake that beckons at our doorstep hasn't changed since French explorer Daniel Greysolon Sieur du Lhut arrived by canoe in 1679.

The pages that follow are a look back, yes. But they're also a look ahead, a look at the possibilities held by a limitless future.

The pages that follow are the way we were.

The way we are.

Chuck Frederick
Duluth News Tribune

Our archival postcard is from Janet Taylor Lewis of Duluth. *Then & Now* staff had never seen an image like this, which bears the inscription: "Balloon view: Harbor, river and natural breakwater: Duluth to the left, Superior to right." In smaller type it says, "No. 19. V.O. Hammon Pub. Co., Minneapolis."

Pat Maus, archivist for the Northeast Minnesota Historical Center, found that the V.O. Hammon Publishing Co. of Minneapolis was in operation from 1904-23. So the rendering of this bird's-eye view may be from the 1800s — there are no buildings — but the postcard was published later.

Maus thinks the image may have been an advertising vehicle for an early 20th-century land developer trying to show how attractive the Northland was to prospective buyers.

The 1979 aerial view of the Duluth side of the harbor obviously is not the same vantage point, but it shows the development that followed in subsequent decades.

Duluth News Tribune
Then & Now
March 8, 2004

This photograph was lent to the *News Tribune* by Bob Hookland of Duluth, who bought it at an estate sale.

It was first thought to be the beginnings of Mesaba Avenue being carved out of the Point of Rocks. When we took the photo to the Duluth Public Works Department to find more information, engineers compared it to a similar photo they had, circa 1918, from 14th Avenue West and Superior Street — several blocks west of Mesaba Avenue.

Another clue to the location was the steeple… (looking east), then located at 11th Avenue West and Superior Street.

Engineering technician Bob Forbort said that the photo shows workers drilling rock, preparing to blast along Superior Street. It is thought that, at some point, an attempt was made to blast straight back to have Superior Street run a straight line. The project was never completed — as today's photo shows.

Duluth News Tribune
Then & Now
March 8, 2000

The loveliness of Lincoln Park in springtime is as evident today as a century ago. Our archival photograph was taken from a book, "Lake Superior and Other Poems," by Will J. Massingham, self-published by its author in 1904.

Bud and Agnes Blackmore found the 190-page book of poems and photographs in the home of Bud's parents, Sidney and Katherine Doran Blackmore, who were the original owners of Duluth's Granada Theater. An inscription on the inside reads "K.E. Doran 1909."

The archival photo looks across Miller Creek to the homes on 25th Avenue West between Third and Fourth streets and to the spire of the old Zion Norwegian Lutheran Church, completed in 1890. Founded by Norwegian immigrants, the church altered its name in 1932 and dedicated a new church building, at 2431 W. Third St., on June 1, 1952.

This year, Zion Lutheran Church will celebrate 50 years in what many congregants still call "the New Zion."

The same century-old homes that are visible in the old photo continue to grace the avenue across from beautiful Lincoln Park.

Duluth News Tribune
Then & Now
May 29, 2002

Our old photograph of the Board of Trade Building comes from a book, "Gibson's Duluth 1901," loaned to the *News Tribune* by Bill Harris of Duluth. Note the horses and wagons on the avenue.

Nearly a full century spans the two photographs. The Board of Trade Building, at the corner of Third Avenue West and First Street, was already six years old in 1901.

The Duluth Board of Trade was organized in 1881 with 12 members, who met for an hour a day to establish prices and market grain. Its original building, built in 1885 on Superior Street, served as communications headquarters for the grain trade until it was destroyed by fire Feb. 10, 1894.

A new site was found on First Street. Designed by Oliver G. Traphagen and Francis W. Fitzpatrick, the Board of Trade Building was constructed in 1895. Originally built to house only grain and commodity trade businesses, the trading floor was on the second floor at the top of the stairs, but was relocated to the eighth floor in the early 1900s to accommodate a growing grain trade business.

The redstone carvings on the front were done by O. George Thrana, a Norwegian immigrant who arrived in Duluth in the spring of 1889 at age 17 and set to work. Today, the work of this sculptor and master stone carver adorns many public buildings, churches, schools and residences in Duluth, and the state capitol in St. Paul. Thrana, also the founder of the Normanna Male Chorus, died in 1939.

In 1901, only seven companies utilized the trade center. By 1912, there were approximately 50 companies represented there. Trading on the floor ceased in 1969 and the Board of Trade dissolved in 1972. The trading floor was vacant until it was remodeled for the Minnesota Ballet in 1999. The original character of the ballroom-like space was not lost and now resembles the grand ballet spaces of Europe.

In addition to a beauty salon and a deli-bakery-catering service, the Board of Trade Building now houses a multitude of businesses — from architects and engineers to telephone service companies and credit unions. A few remaining businesses deal with grain trading, such as S.A. McLennan Co. and Daniels Shipping Service.

Although he's no longer affiliated with the operation of the Board of Trade Building, Dennis Lamkin, senior leasing manager with U.S. Bank Corporate Properties, managed the property for some 20 years and has become an unofficial building historian.

Only once was the building

threatened, Lamkin said. On June 4, 1948, a fire that began across the street at Rudolph's Furniture Factory threatened buildings nearby and trade was suspended for a day. Had it not been for the heroic efforts of maintenance man Lloyd Houck, the entire Board of Trade Building likely would have gone up in flames. Houck went from space to space with a fire hose, extinguishing the burning window frames. The ornate cornice, which originally adorned the building, was badly damaged during the fire and had to be replaced with the flat cornice now in place.

Duluth News Tribune
Then & Now
Nov. 15, 2000

This image is similar to one shared by Howard and Lee Gyllen of Duluth from a laminated place mat. The image shows the city's landmark bridge, built in 1905 as a trolley system rather than a lift bridge.

Quoting from the place mat: "This wonderful tribute to American genius is built across the Government Piers, a span of 393 feet high from the water line.

"The only bridge of its kind in the world…it may be likened to the trolley system used in stores to transport packages from the counter to the wrapping desk. Cost of construction was $1 million.

"Modeled after the suspended traveling bridge at Rouen, France, it consisted of an overhead span of riveted steel supported by high towers and a rigidly suspended, electrically operated car (34 by 50 feet) which ran back and forth on cables.

The trip from one side of the channel to the other was made in one minute at a speed of four miles to eight miles an hour."

With more people owning automobiles in the 1920s, a quicker transit system across the channel necessitated a different kind of bridge. The Aerial Lift Bridge was built in 1930 and underwent a major overhaul the winter of 1999-2000.

Today's view, taken Feb. 5, 2004, shows a snow-filled landscape.

Duluth News Tribune
Then & Now
April 5, 2004

On June 25, 1892, Duluthians turned out in force for the dedication of a site for a new post office on First Street between Fourth and Fifth avenues west. The festivities are pictured at right.

Earlier postal facilities had been small, wooden buildings resembling — and sometimes originally used as — one-room schoolhouses. The old building pictured, across from the current site of the *News Tribune*, was an immense castle-like brownstone that served as the central Duluth post office from 1894 to 1930.

The magnificent building was razed after completion of a

new federal building, which today is the site of the Civic Center Post Office. That building, at the far west side of the Civic Center courtyard, was the main post office until 1970, when the current headquarters opened at 27th Avenue West and Michigan Street.

Today's view looks along First Street toward City Hall.

Duluth News Tribune
Then & Now
June 5, 2002

R onald Rosicky of Cromwell helped us with the caption for our *Then & Now* photos, which show early views of Cromwell as well as the town today.

Our oldest photo shows Main Street in Cromwell in the early 1900s. The view looks west from the east end of town. Clockwise from left are Violets's Hotel and the pool hall on the left side and Hill's Store and Morse's store on the right side of the photo.

Our second archival photo, obviously from a later period, shows vintage automobiles parked along Cromwell's Main Street. The view this time looks east toward the south side of the street. Cromwell's first post office is at the far left, a house (which still stands) is toward the center and Violet's Hotel and

the Pool Hall, located downstairs in a building labeled "General Merchandising," complete the scene.

Today's view looks west from Cromwell's first post office (at far left in photo). Along the right side of the photo are several businesses, including The Trolley Store & Station and the Country Café.

Duluth News Tribune
Then & Now
Dec. 4, 2002

This *News Tribune* file photograph of Gary-New Duluth is dated Dec. 5, 1978.

The building at far left is gone now, but Shear Delight Hair Styling, at 1412 Commonwealth Ave., is in the small, wooden building where Casual Beauty Salon was located in 1978. The numbers go down as one looks toward Fond du Lac.

The 1978 city directory lists 1336 Commonwealth as vacant. The Congress Bar & Grill was and still is at 1334 Commonwealth. Frank's Barber Shop was at 1330; Running Brothers Siding was at 1328; Flowers North was at 1318; Delores' Café was at 1314; Ace High Tavern was at 1308 and the Far West Market at 1306. At 1302 is the Gary Dental Building and Duluth Western Credit Union. Also visible across the street in the old picture are two service stations — a Phillips 66/Milkhouse at 1331 and a Gary Skelly gas station at 1301.

The 2003 city directory lists some of those same addresses as follows: Puglisi's Gun Emporium is at 1336 Commonwealth; Congress Bar & Grill at 1334; Alpine Bar at 1308; Moose Lodge 1478 at 1306; Creative Cutz Salon (beauty salon) at 1302. Across the street where the service stations formerly sat, the directory lists the Milkhouse at 1331 and a Little Store at 1301 Commonwealth.

Duluth News Tribune
Then & Now
April 19, 2004

B ill Harris of Duluth brought in his copy of "Gibson's 1901 Duluth," a souvenir booklet published by the city's Commercial Club.

Inside, we found this photograph of the Duluth Brewing and Malting Co. The brewery was established in 1896 at 29th Avenue West and Helm Street. Owners Charles Meeske, Reiner Hoch and E.N. Breitung had been formerly associated with a Marquette, Mich., bottling company. By 1900, a malting plant and other expansions were added to the original structure.

According to "Duluth, Sketches of the Past," published by the American Revolution Bicentennial Commission in 1976, the brewing company produced "soft drinks and cereal beverages during the early years of Prohibition" but was inactive between 1928 and 1933. After that, Duluth Brewing and Malt Co. produced Karlsbad beer and "was one of only 10 breweries in the United States that produced malt for its own use and sold the excess. Hamm's of St. Paul was the only other Minnesota brewery to do so. The company later produced Royal Bohemian and Royal 58 brand beers and also made Salisbury brand carbonated water."

In the post-World War II years, in cooperation with another company, Duluth Brewing and Malt Co. again produced soft drinks — this time under the Lovit brand name.

The company closed in 1952 but was rehabilitated and reopened in 1960. It closed permanently a few years later.

In today's view, cars, trucks and SUVs rush along the I-35 freeway past the site where the brewery once stood.

Duluth News Tribune
Then & Now
April 18, 2001

Our archival postcard is described as an "aerial view of Denfeld High School, Duluth, Minnesota." A local card collector shared a story he had heard about the school's design but admitted it may be a myth.

The original plan, he was told, was to extend the west side of the school so that, from the air, the shape of the facility would resemble a block "D." Not so, according to the book, "Duluth's Legacy: Architecture, Vol. 1." It says architects Hosltead and Sullivan, inspired by Ivy League schools whose symbolism represented academic discipline and idealism, designed the school with its tower, beautiful auditorium and classic architecture, in an "H" shape.

At any rate, Denfeld High School, at 44th Avenue West and Fourth Street, first opened to almost 900 students in grades 10-12 in the 1926-27 school year.

It was not the first school by that name. A decade earlier, in 1915, a new high school on North Central Avenue had been built and named after local educational leader and longtime superintendent of Duluth public schools Robert E. Denfeld. But World War I spurred growth in West Duluth to the point that a larger facility was necessary. That original "Denfeld" on Central Avenue, just 11 years old, served

for many years as West Junior High School and later became Laura MacArthur Elementary School.

Denfeld High School cost $1.25 million to build, a handsome sum in that era, and its beauty is still a source of community pride. For nearly 20 years, Denfeld was also home to the Duluth Junior College, an alternative for high school graduates who did not go on to the Duluth State Teachers College.

Duluth News Tribune
Then & Now
Dec. 1, 2003

Built in 1908, Ensign School, at 1013 Piedmont Ave., provided an elementary education for generations of West End (now called Lincoln Park) children. The two-story brick building, with a playground/skating rink beside it, held 10 classrooms for kindergarten through sixth grade and had its own library.

The building was named for Judge Josiah Davis Ensign, who served as judge of the juvenile court in Duluth.

Pat Maus, archivist for the Northeast Minnesota Historical Center in the University of Minnesota Duluth Library, dug up the following information about New York-born, Ohio-bred Ensign. He was admitted to the Ohio bar in 1853 at age 20 and was elected clerk of courts for Jefferson County. He taught school, was appointed county auditor and entered law practice. In 1865, he and his wife, Kate, took a steamer on the Great Lakes; they were bound for St. Paul. While aboard, Ensign heard Duluth described by U.S. Sen. Henry M. Rice of St. Paul as "not exceeding four houses, no hotel and…a party of 14 exceeded the whole white population."

A few years later, by then a widower, Ensign came to Duluth to practice law. He also filled a vacancy on the Duluth School Board, where he remained in service for seven years. He remarried in 1872 and held many public offices, including county attorney, mayor in 1882 and village president. He served as a district court judge for 32 years (1889-1921) and was Duluth's first "juvenile judge."

He loved children. It became an annual event for the children of Ensign School to send him bouquets of flowers on his birthday. This was the 88-year-old Ensign's reply to them in 1921, two years before his death:

"My dear children. I am at a loss to frame words that adequately express my delight in receiving the birthday present you sent me of two baskets of the earliest spring flowers — not growing in a garden or a hothouse but…made beautiful by nature's own hand. Someone said that flowers are the smiles of children and I thank you

for searching for, and gathering for me these first smiles of spring…In youth we learn; in later years, we practice what we have learned. How important it is that you should be in all things prepared for whatever you may encounter in your mature years.

"Most sincerely, gratefully yours, J.D. Ensign."

The high esteem with which he was regarded is illustrated by quoting President William H. Taft (1909-13), then chief justice of the U.S. Supreme Court, who — after talking with Judge Ensign — said: "It was worth crossing the continent to meet him."

The Duluth Herald reported Nov. 30, 1923: "Through his work as judge of juvenile court, he grew to know and love children. Therefore selecting a name for one of its public schools, Duluth felt no one was more worthy of having his name perpetuated."

Ensign School was remodeled in 1929. It closed on June 8, 1979, and was burned by arsonists Feb. 20, 1981. The lot where the elementary school stood for more than 70 years now houses several dwellings.

Duluth News Tribune
Then & Now
Dec. 5, 2001

Our archival photograph is from a booklet, "Early Days in Duluth," published by Stewart-Taylor Co. of Duluth, which credits its contents to the St. Louis County Historical Society and the Duluth Public Library.

The photo's caption reads: "Fargusson Building, 402 W. Superior St." It is probably from the late 1800s.

According to Pat Maus, archivist for the Northeast Minnesota Historical Center, the 1888-89 city directory lists "Thomas Dowse, real estate" at 402 W. Superior St. and "Charles Schiller Wholesale and Retail Cigar, Tobacco and Smokers' Articles," at 404 W. Superior St.

Maus also noted that the directory listed Albert Schiller as clerk at the tobacco establishment. Maus thinks Albert may have been a brother or a son because both Charles and Albert are listed as residing at 26 W. Superior St. The wagon in front of Schiller-Hubbard Co. appears to be a "company car." Advertising on the side touts Lorillard's chewing tobacco and imported Key West cigars.

The horses and buggies are long gone, but businesses at Fourth Avenue West today include Trip Planners, a travel agency specializing in leisure and corporate travel, at 400 W. Superior St. (on the corner) and Renegade Comedy Theatre at 404 W. Superior St. The storefront at 402 W. Superior St. is vacant.

Duluth News Tribune
Then & Now
Jan. 8, 2003

The *Duluth News Tribune* archival photograph is labeled "First Avenue East and Second Street looking east." A question mark follows what appears to be a guess of "circa 1875."

We don't know who the photographer was or why that specific part of town was photographed. According to Pat Maus of the Northeast Minnesota Historical Center, the first city directory was produced in 1882.

The center has a similar photograph by Paul B. Gaylord that identifies the church at left as "the first Congregational church (in Duluth), at the northeast corner of First Avenue East and Second Street." It identifies the church off in the background as "the Presbyterian at Third Avenue East."

Maus knows that both of those 19th-century churches were on the upper side of East Second Street.

Started in 1869 and completed in 1871 at the corner of Second Street and Third Avenue East, the Presbyterian church was Duluth's first church building. It later became the Finnish Lutheran Church.

In 1892, the congregation of First Presbyterian relocated and built a large brownstone structure, which still stands at 300 E. Second St.

Today's view looks down Second Street from First Avenue East.

Duluth News Tribune
Then & Now
March 13, 2002

ENGER PARK MUNICIPAL GOLF COURSE, DULUTH, MINN   746-30

Archival postcards of the Enger Golf Clubhouse were submitted by several readers.

The nine-hole Enger Municipal Golf Course opened July 2, 1927. Duluth's first public course came about as a gift several years earlier from F.J. Enger, president of the Enger & Olson Furniture Co., who asked the city to develop the land for recreational purposes.

But finding information about the course and its history was a challenge until Scott Heger, golf professional, directed *Then & Now* to Nancy Jensen, widow of Hank Jensen.

Hank Jensen caddied at the course on opening day in 1927. He became a PGA golf pro in the late 1940s and served as Enger's golf professional and manager for over a quarter-century.

Nancy Jensen shared treasured photographs and articles from scrapbooks, including several descriptions in 1927 of "the new clubhouse at Enger Park just completed at a cost of $12,000." Originally facing a different direction and located at the site of today's 18th hole, the clubhouse was moved about 200 yards to its present site in 1941.

The 50th anniversary of Enger Golf Course was celebrated July 2, 1977, drawing some 275 players to celebrate the occasion. Like opening day five decades earlier, it was a Saturday.

Duluth News Tribune
Then & Now
July 28, 2003

Marjorie Oustad of Duluth says her maternal grandfather, Henry Britton, was a camera buff. He and Oustad's older sister, Jane Catlin, posed for this photograph, circa 1925, at the site of the old Endion train station on South Street below London Road.

The tiny depot was right across the street from Britton's home at 330 S. 15th Ave. E., a boardinghouse run by his wife, Maud Britton.

Today the area looks quite different because the freeway has taken most of the land beneath South Street, where the tiny depot once stood. But the roof lines of many of the same homes are still in the picture — 75 years later.

Duluth News Tribune
Then & Now
May 17, 2000

Nancy Otos of Duluth took a picture of the Fountain Drive-In on Woodland Avenue in 1959 or 1960, when she dreamed of working there.

Otos thinks the server in the window is her friend Pauline Morrow Davies, eldest daughter of Ray Morrow, who opened the drive-in at what was then called "the end of the Woodland car line."

Otos remembers that one of the greatest disappointments in her teen life — she was a 1961 Duluth East graduate — was not being hired to work at the drive-in.

In the photograph, Pauline Morrow is serving another Duluth East classmate (and Fountain employee), Sandy Andreson, now Sandy Hawkins. Note the sign: 19 cents bought either a hamburger or a shake.

Morrow named the establishment the Fountain because he had plans, and drawings to prove it, that would feature a grand fountain out in front. He never did add it because the place got so busy.

One of the reasons the drive-in enjoyed such success was that Morrow had tasted Col. Harlan Sanders' chicken in Minneapolis and bought the Duluth franchise of Kentucky Fried Chicken for the Fountain. His wife, Helen, specialized in cooking the chicken and all five daughters worked at the Fountain.

Morrow dreamed of opening a strip mall at the site but couldn't get financial backing to do it.

Today, several businesses are in the area where the Fountain thrived. They include Falk's Woodland Pharmacy at 1 Calvary Road, Denny's Ace Hardware at 7 Calvary Road and Denny's Lawn & Garden at 4122 Woodland Ave.

Duluth News Tribune
Then & Now
Dec. 18, 2002

While visiting Duluth, Karen Torgerson of Lansing, Ill., brought in this 1888 photograph of a funeral in progress on Third Street between Eighth and Ninth avenues east.

"In the casket being carried from the house is my great-grandmother, Maria Christina (Nilsen) Torgerson, who died Oct. 22, 1888, in Duluth of asthma," Torgerson wrote.

Maria's death at age 26 left her husband, Gunder M. Torgerson, and a six-month-old son, Levi. Many of the family's descendants still live in Duluth. Gunder later married Ingeborg Boe and they had four daughters.

The funeral cortege is lined up outside 821 E. Third St., then home to Gunder "Gust" and Maria "Mary" Torgerson, who had been married in 1886 in the Norwegian Lutheran Church in Duluth. A Norwegian immigrant, Gunder was a carpenter by trade and may have built the home himself. In subsequent years, he constructed numerous homes on the East Hillside.

Karen Torgerson thinks the infant in white held by someone on the porch is Levi, Karen's grandfather, who grew up to be a building contractor and also constructed numerous homes on the East Hillside and in the University of Minnesota Duluth area.

The 1880s were a period of intense growthin Duluth. An 1885 state census cites the population as 18,036. Five years later, the federal census of 1890 noted the population had increased to 33,115.

Duluth News Tribune
Then & Now
Aug. 11, 2003

The oldest photograph of that marvelous "House of Rocks" on Skyline Drive came to us via Bob Kunze, who lives there now and enjoys memorabilia of the historic home that he and his wife bought in 1980.

Kunze acquired the photo from George Cook Jr., grandson of the home's original owner, Arthur Purdon Cook. The photo shows A.P. Cook standing on the rock stairway as it was being built between 1902 and 1904.

The picture below, actually a penny postcard, came to us courtesy of Ray Zierhut of Cass Lake, who wrote: "When my uncle returned from France after World War I, he lived in Duluth for a while. He was the one who collected these cards. So I figure they date back to the late teens or early 1920s. My dear mother has saved them all these years." The postcard is captioned "House and Rock Garden on Skyline Drive, Duluth, Minn."

The third photo reflects the venerable house today. Owners Bob and Kit Kunze are the fifth owners.

Kunze, a high school teacher and basketball coach, grew up in Duluth's Central Hillside and his wife, a U.S. Postal Service worker, was raised in the Norton Park area. When they learned that the landmark house at 501 W. Skyline Parkway was for sale early in 1980, they merely wanted to see how it looked inside. They didn't expect to actually buy it, but an enterprising real estate agent's persistence paid off. Once they sealed the deal, they got in touch with Cook's family and began to collect information

122-D House and Rock Garden on Skyline Drive, Duluth, Minn.

about the home's history.

Knowing that past owners felt close to the dwelling, they invited widow Eleanor Storms for a visit. She and her husband, Wesley, had owned the house from the early 1940s until the 1970s.

Known to generations of Duluthians as a landmark on the boulevard, the house was designed by I. Vernon Hill as the home for A.P. Cook, who had come to Duluth in 1884 as a young druggist. Eventually, he acquired wealth

and influence. At one time he was the secretary for the St. Louis County Poor Commission, which operated the poorhouse.

According the Kunze, the home is 30 feet by 50 feet on the main level; the upstairs has about 800 square feet.

"In Realtor terms, a story and a half," Kunze said. Basement foundation walls are Duluth bluestone. Fifty-seven steps lead to the basement, and most of the rocks in the staircase leading to the house are original, Kunze said. The couple has replaced some missing rocks and added a cable car on the side of the house.

With the help of their three children they have put Christmas lights in the windows and on the staircase. They don't mind people stopping to look at their house any time of year, Kunze said.

"In summer, all you have to do is sit in a lawn chair to see how many people stop to look at it," he said.

Duluth News Tribune
Then & Now
Dec. 20, 2000

Grace Chesny of Duluth found our old photograph — a postcard — among her father's old albums. The sepia-colored card, circa the early 1920s, reads "Ridgeview Golf Club, Duluth, Minn."

According to Pat Maus at the Northeast Minnesota Historical Center, the private Ridgeview Golf Club's 18-hole golf course, at the end of West Winona Road in the Woodland neighborhood, opened in 1922. The first women's annual championship tournament was played in August 1929 and won by Mrs. F.E. Boyd.

The two municipal courses in that era were Enger (18 holes) and Lester Park. Lester Park's 18-hole golf course opened in 1931. At that time, there were two other private clubs, Northland (established in 1904, it expanded to 18 holes in 1912) at 39th Avenue East and Superior Street and Riverside (nine holes) at 85th Avenue West.

Our current photo shows the clubhouse of the 160-acre Ridgeview Country Club, which today has about 325 members. The general manager is Phil Gaudino.

According to course superintendent Wes Salo, Ridgeview was designed as an 18-hole golf course. Hole No. 12 was relocated in the 1940s. In 1988, holes 2, 9, 13 and 17 were relocated. All ponds were added in 1988. The course is now under construction for redesign of hole No. 15.

Duluth News Tribune
Then & Now
Dec. 11, 2002

This photograph of the Lyceum Theater and Office Building is taken from a book, "Gibson's Souvenir of Duluth 1901," loaned to the *News Tribune* by Bill Harris of Duluth.

The Lyceum stood at the present site of KDLH-TV/Channel 3, between Fourth and Fifth Avenues west on Superior Street.

According to "Duluth's Legacy: Architecture, Vol. 1," "the opening of the Lyceum in 1891 was a star occasion in the career of the newly-formed partnership" of architects Oliver G. Traphagen and Francis W. Fitzpatrick. A year earlier, they had been commissioned by sawmill and railroad magnate Andreas Miller to design the Romanesque building later called the "handsomest and costliest building in the region."

By July 1891, the Lyceum was ready to be occupied. Six stories high, seven at the corners, it possessed the largest stage area in the Midwest — with the exception of a Chicago theater. Another interesting aspect of the lavish sandstone and brick structure was that it was declared "absolutely fireproof" and, throughout its life, lived up to that claim.

A little-known piece of Lyceum history was revealed several years ago when the *News Tribune*'s Eh? column carried the following item: "Turns out that July 13, 1936 — the hottest day in Duluth history — is red-letter for another reason as well. On that day, those zany Marx Brothers arrived in town to perform a stage version of their script for 'A Day At the Races' at the Lyceum Theater. Groucho, Harpo and Chico (Zeppo was gone by then) were on a four-city tour to test their coming film's jokes and musical numbers on an audience." The newspaper credited folks at Renegade Comedy Theatre for digging up that bit of history. Renegade, at 424 W. Superior St., is located directly across the street from where the Lyceum once stood.

Veteran *News Tribune* staffer James Heffernan was a young reporter in February 1966 when the venerable building was about to be razed. Tours were offered and visitors received fliers containing newspaper reports of the Lyceum's lavish opening 75 years earlier. Heffernan wrote a mock obituary for the Lyceum, which was published in the *Duluth Herald* (the afternoon paper) the following day.

In part it read: "In a colorful career which saw her transition from lavish stage productions to Hollywood films — two at a time for 50 cents — the Lyceum (stayed alive) …despite the advent of television and a more mobile population, which…sought other forms of entertainment." Heffernan attributed the Lyceum's death to "urban renewal illness," citing Duluth theaters which had, by that time, been torn down or stood vacant. "She was preceded in death by the Garrick, Lyric, Strand, Lake, Doric, Star and Lakeside Art." He listed "survivors" in 1966 as her "three sisters, the NorShor, Granada and West." Only the NorShor remains today.

A plaque on the corner of Fifth Avenue West and Superior Street commemorates the theater, which occupied that block for three-quarters of a century. Sculpted carvings of the faces of comedy and tragedy, which once graced the theater's entrance, now grace the entry to the Duluth Playhouse auditorium.

Duluth News Tribune
Then & Now
March 21, 2001

The two-story stucco building on the corner of 24th Avenue West and Piedmont Avenue was built in 1914. At first, it was an ice cream parlor and confectionery patronized by the hikers along Miller Creek in the mile-long Lincoln Park.

In 1919, it was purchased by the John and Jenny Lundquist family, whose Central Laundry in Cloquet had been destroyed by the 1918 Cloquet fire. Over the years, it has been a general grocery store, hardware store and gas station. John Lundquist Sr. is shown pumping gas.

During World War II, the building was sold and moved south — to 1315 Piedmont Ave. Today, the building is home to Electric Systems of Duluth, an electrical contractor for residential and commercial wiring. The company's owners, Dave Michalski, Clint Johnson and Charles Hanson, purchased the building about 15 years ago.

The former site of the Lundquist establishment is now home to a Food-N-Fuel Mobil convenience store at 1323 Piedmont Ave. It is owned and operated by Curtis Oil Co.

Information about the old facility was provided by John Lundquist Jr., 86, the youngest of John and Jenny Lundquist's seven children, who lives in a retirement condominium in St. Clair, Mich.

Duluth News Tribune
Then & Now
Jan. 10, 2001

Our archival photograph of Munger Terrace was taken from a book, "Lake Superior and Other Poems," by Will J. Massingham, self-published in 1904. Bud and Agnes Blackmore of Duluth found the 190-page book of poems and photographs in the home of Bud's parents, Sidney and Katherine Doran Blackmore.

According to the 1974 book, "Duluth's Legacy: Architecture, Vol. 1," in 1891 Duluth architects Traphagen and Fitzpatrick designed eight dwelling units of 16 rooms each for Roger S. Munger to rent. Munger's Victorian home stood nearby. The book continues, "When Munger Terrace opened, the newly formed Sacred Heart Academy (forerunner of Villa Scholastica) rented quarters in the building until 1895. Munger Terrace was the place to live but by 1915 the place (to live) was the East End, and the eight apartments were subdivided into 32."

Today the building at 405 Mesaba Ave. continues to serve as an apartment building.

Duluth News Tribune
Then & Now
Jan. 15, 2003

1869–Minnesota Point from Lake Avenue and 2nd Street

Our old photograph was included in a book, "Early Days in Duluth," published by Stewart Taylor Co. The photo was labeled "1869 — Minnesota Point from Lake Avenue and Second Street."

The photo also depicts the first St. Paul's Episcopal Church, built in 1869, at the northwest corner of Lake Avenue and Second Street. One of our now photos looks toward Minnesota Point from that location today. The third photo shows the present St. Paul's Episcopal Church, at 1710 E. Superior St.

Designed by Bertram Goodhue of New York in 1912, the present St. Paul's was designed in the manner of an English country parish church. The book "Duluth's Legacy: Architecture, Vol. 1" says about the church: "The warm stone, soft moldings and tracery and fine blue-gray slate roof gently stress its Gothic heritage." The book

said a 1929 addition cost $105,000 while the church's main portion had cost $72,000.

The Rev. Howard Anderson, rector of St. Paul's, said that today the church serves a congregation of about 1,200 members. Its five clergy are committed to its mission statement: "St. Paul's — a place for everyone and a ministry for everyone." That includes serving the East Hillside neighborhood with projects such as Little Treasures Child Care Center, a computer lab primarily serving neighborhood children and elders and programs for neighbors moving from welfare to work.

Duluth News Tribune
Then & Now
Dec. 25, 2002

T his postcard bearing the inscription, "McDougall Terminal Building, Duluth, Minn," was sent by John Ebeling of Bloomington, Minn.

Its sweeping view of the harbor includes a view of the landmark Aerial Bridge when it was not yet a lift bridge. From construction in 1905 until 1929, when the bridge was redesigned, a basket carried cargo back and forth across the canal linking downtown Duluth with the Park Point peninsula.

Pat Maus, archivist of the Northeast Minnesota Historical Center, found some background on the McDougall Terminal. Named for Scotsman, inventor, patent holder, financier and shipbuilder Capt. Alexander McDougall (1845-1923), the building's first unit was completed in 1923.

McDougall's son, A. Miller McDougall, born in Duluth in 1884, served as president of the McDougall Terminal and Warehouse Co.

The elder McDougall was inducted posthumously into the Great Lakes Hall of Fame in Sault St. Marie, Mich., in 1968 and in 1982 into the National Maritime Hall of Fame at the U.S. Merchant Marine Academy in Kings Point, N.Y.

Maus said what most people will recall about McDougall is that he was the inventor of the whaleback vessel. The only whaleback that still exists is the S.S. Meteor in Superior.

Duluth News Tribune
Then & Now
Jan. 12, 2004

Our old photograph was rescued by Beryl Gilbertson of Duluth when a friend was about to toss some old things out. This print is dated on the back May 4, 1925.

Another *Then and Now* reader, who worked on the waterfront for years, says it looks like a tug is towing a string of barges — with another tug in the rear holding them in alignment while passing through the ship canal. He noted that

the bridge on Minnesota Point had not yet become a lift bridge.

Visible in the photograph are other elements of a bygone era — the freight sheds used for either shipping or railroad.

Today's view looks toward the Aerial Lift Bridge, one of Duluth's most well-known landmarks.

Duluth News Tribune
Then & Now
May 8, 2002

Two views of Minnesota Slip depict changing times over a century.

The first view of the slip is from a 1904 publication "Lake Superior and Other Poems," loaned to the *News Tribune* by Bud and Agnes Blackmore of Duluth. Note Central High School's clock tower in the background.

Today's view of Minnesota Slip shows the S.S. William A. Irvin ore boat, a visitor attraction permanently docked there.

For 40 years, from 1938 to 1978, the S.S. William A. Irvin carried iron ore and coal to Great Lakes ports. As the proud flagship of U.S. Steel's Great Lakes Fleet, she provided comfort and elegance to dignitaries and guests who traveled the lakes with her. The Irvin was added to the National Register of Historic Places in 1989.

Duluth News Tribune
Then & Now
June 12, 2002

Our archival photograph was sent to us by Robert Johnsted of Superior. The photo is on the cover of a Minnesota Historical Rail Calendar, which Johnsted collected throughout the 1980s until Blue River Publications of Rochester, Minn., quit producing them. The 1983 version, which contained this image, was "a photo collection of Minnesota's most famous steam locomotives."

Its calendar caption reads, in part: "The classic steam era photograph by Marvin Neilsen brings back all the marvelous memories of the great steam locomotive.

"Leaving Duluth for Chicago is the Omaha Road's train 513. To the left is the Omaha Road Depot, one of three major downtown depots in Duluth."

The early 1950s cars in the photo tell us this must have been shot near the end of the steam locomotive era. Visible in the background are the Crane Co. and Rust-Parker buildings as well as the Marshall-Wells water tower.

The "now" photograph shows a different world, one where the automobile is king and Interstate 35 is its castle. Off in the distance at right, the water tower is still a landmark. Beneath it today is Hawthorn Suites, the hotel created within the old Marshall-Wells facility that incorporates much of the original architecture into its design.

Duluth News Tribune
Then & Now
March 5, 2003

jon helstrom

O ur two archival photographs — one is an architect's drawing — are courtesy of Erling Breivik of Duluth. He was superintendent of the last major construction and renovation of the Providence Building in the early 1980s and acquired them from project architect Jon Helstrom. We think the earlier photo is also a renovation.

On Sept. 21, 1912, the *Duluth Herald* featured a story about two additional stories being added to the 1895 building. Barely visible in the upper left corner of the picture at far left is the Alworth Building, built in 1910. In that era, the St. Louis Hotel occupied the space between the Alworth and the Providence — where the Medical Arts Building, completed in 1933, now stands. Breivik noted that the Providence Building's distinctive oval-shaped windows were removed during the 1980s renovation. At the same time, the main entryway was moved toward the east. A stairwell on the west side of the building (seen in the 1912 photo leading to the basement) was closed up in the 1960s, according to Breivik. Note the long dresses of the women on the sidewalk and the horses and buggies parked on Fourth Avenue West. A Northern Pacific Railroad office is located on the first floor. Breivik said that a central fire vault of clay tile and steel doors that reached to the top floor of the building was removed during that 1980s project.

Today, the Providence Building is home to many businesses and managed by Upper Midwest Management Corp. of Minneapolis.

Duluth News Tribune
Then & Now
Jan. 22, 2003

Roma Riehle of Grand Rapids sent a digital image of our old photograph, which looks down at Rice's Point from an unidentified location in the 1800s. The photograph is half of a stereoscope slide.

Riehle wrote: "The half slide is mounted on cardboard and seems to be a sepia-toned print. On the edge of the print, it states 'Scenery at the Head of Lake Superior, P.B. Gaylord, Photographer, Duluth, Minn.'"

Riehle notes that the photo was the property of her grandparents, Henry L. and Nellie (Widger) Smith. Her grandmother came to Duluth in 1868 with her parents aboard the St. Paul, the first time that boat came to Duluth. On board was Engine No. 5, the first engine put on the Lake Superior & Mississippi Railroad, later called the St. Paul and Duluth Railroad. Nellie Widger later married Smith, one of the first engineers on the railroad.

According to the 1976 bicentennial publication "Duluth Sketches of the Past," Rice's Point was so named because Orrin Wheeler Rice filed a claim for a site on the jutting peninsula between the harbor and St. Louis Bay in 1854. He and his brother-in-law built a house on the site that became Garfield Avenue.

Because of buildings and foliage blocking the view elsewhere, today's view of Rice's Point was photographed from the Enger Tower overlook.

Duluth News Tribune
Then & Now
Sept. 15, 2003

A nita Bloom of Hermantown was the source of this archival photo that shows her father, Arthur "Art" E. Holmberg, in the cab of a Rust-Parker truck, probably in the early 1940s. Holmberg is talking to company manager Bill Olson. The truck's Fruehauf trailer was reportedly Duluth's first "semi."

Rust-Parker, a wholesale grocery company, was located at 217 Lake Ave. S. along with Griggs Cooper & Co., a wholesale liquor distributor. Bloom recalled that the parking lot of Rust-Parker was next to the slip of water where the William A. Irvin is now anchored.

The old photo faces north, toward downtown Duluth where the backsides of George A. Hormel & Co., 14 W. Michigan St., and Duluth Paper Co., 18 W. Michigan St., are visible.

The "now" photo, taken from the front parking lot of the Red Lobster Restaurant at 301 S. Lake Ave., faces the opposite direction (toward the canal) and emphasizes the growth of diverse businesses in the former warehouse district. There is no longer a structure where Rust-Parker stood. KBJR-TV Channel 6 studio is at 246 Lake Ave. S., across the avenue. Other businesses along Lake Avenue South in the old warehouse district include Canal Park Liquor, Silver Creek Traders, Blue Lake Gallery, Canal Park Antiques, Hawthorn Suites and Timber Lodge Steakhouse, Old Chicago, Green Mill Restaurant, Canal Park Pets, Subway, Lake Avenue Café and a host of other businesses in the DeWitt-Seitz Marketplace at 394 S. Lake Ave.

Duluth News Tribune
Then & Now
Nov. 29, 2000

Nancy Aanonsen of Duluth donated this and other postcards to the *News Tribune*, requesting that we mention they were given to her by the late Anna Nelson of Hermantown, who was a neighbor.

The Nelsons, Anna and her husband, Bernard, owned and operated Nelson's Coffee Shop on the corner of Highway 194 and Miller Trunk Highway. While our copy is a sepia-tone, the originals were full-color, oversized postcards which were sold at the restaurant.

Aanonsen and Nelson used to sit and have coffee when Aanonsen brought in her neighbor's mail. Nelson gave the postcards to Aanonsen, saying she hoped she'd find a use for them.

The late 1930s automobiles, parked on Skyline Parkway, give some indication of when this 7- by 10-inch postcard photograph was taken.

The 1940 bird's-eye view of Duluth was taken from the yard of the "House of Rocks," at 501 W. Skyline Parkway. That home, which today is still a Duluth landmark, was owned by Wesley and Eleanor Storms from the early 1940s into the 1970s.

Portions of downtown visible in the 1940s postcard include the Civic Center; and a few blocks east, on Superior Street, the Lonsdale, Alworth, Torrey and Medical Arts buildings. The population of Duluth was more than 101,000 according to the 1940 census.

Today's view captures the round tower of the Radisson Hotel Duluth-Harborview and Duluth Entertainment Convention Center.

According to information compiled by the Duluth Area Chamber of Commerce, the population of Duluth today is 85,493.

Duluth News Tribune
Then & Now
Jan. 31, 2001

Designed by architect James J. Egan of Chicago, the seven-story, 200-room Spalding Hotel, 428 W. Superior St., was a fixture in Duluth from 1889 until its demolition began on Sept. 25, 1963.

The $350,000 that built the hotel came from Pennsylvania-born William Witter Spalding (1820-1901), who came to Duluth in 1869 and was elected a Duluth city alderman in 1870. He was the first president and a director of the D&IR (Duluth & Iron Range) railway and also the Duluth & Winnipeg Railroad.

According to a newspaper article published the day the demolition began, the nearly 75-year-old hotel was the first facility set for demolition in the Gateway Urban Renewal project, which changed the face of downtown Duluth over the next two decades.

Our archival photographs are from the *News Tribune* files. The photo on the left shows a busy hotel in the 1920s. On the right our 1963 photograph shows a pedestrian walking under the hotel marquee. Across Superior Street and Fifth Avenue West stand the Holland Hotel and other businesses, which would later meet the wrecking ball.

Today, the Ordean Building is at 424 W. Superior St., near the location of the once-regal hotel. The view across Fifth Avenue West today reveals the Radisson Hotel Duluth-Harborview.

Duluth News Tribune
Then & Now
May 1, 2002

J ohn Ebeling of Bloomington, Minn., shares this Superior Street view that he found on a vintage color postcard. Its legend reads, "Superior Street is Duluth's main thoroughfare and, from Seventh Avenue West to Sixth Avenue East, traverses the business district." It continues, "London Road intersects Superior Street and continues along the shore of Lake Superior practically all the way from Duluth to Port Arthur and Fort William, Canada."

The old postcard depicts the Hill Hotel at left (513½ W. Superior St.) and the Saratoga Hotel at right (514-516 W. Superior St.). Visible down the street to the left are the Holland Hotel and, across Fifth Avenue West, the Lyceum Building. The Spalding Hotel resembles a castle on the right. All of those buildings are gone now, much of the area having been razed in the Gateway Urban Renewal project.

Today's view has the Radisson Hotel Duluth-Harborview at left and the Duluth Public Library at right.

Duluth News Tribune
Then & Now
May 10, 2004

Henry A. Hillman Jr. of Mount Serling, Ky., sent a similar photograph in 1939 of the Duluth Incline Railway.

The Incline extended 2,749 feet from Superior Street to Ninth Street along Seventh Avenue West. Riders were offered an unparalleled view of the city as they traversed up or down the hill on its parallel tracks.

A viable tourist attraction from the moment it was built in 1891, "The Incline," as it came to be nicknamed, reportedly was hailed as "a stupendous project that will put the Zenith City on a metropolitan basis."

In 1889, the Highland Improvement Co. was formed with the purpose of plotting and developing what later became Duluth Heights. Getting people to those heights was an early purpose of The Incline.

The late Evelyn Holmberg, a longtime Duluth teacher, recalled riding The Incline regularly in the early 1920s with her siblings and mother, Anna Ofstun. They would debark at the top of the hill and walk from there to visit a friend of Mrs. Ofstun's, who lived in Duluth Heights.

Our current photograph does not attempt to replicate the view from the top of the hill at Seventh Avenue West. Today's view is taken from what we estimate was the approximate location of The Incline tracks in the 300 block of Seventh Avenue West.

Duluth News Tribune
Then & Now
Aug. 15, 2001

R ichard Randall of Duluth brought in a sepia-colored post-card. It depicts Torrance Hall, one of two dormitories for Duluth Normal School, which opened its main building in 1902 at 23rd Avenue East and Fifth Street.

Within a decade, two dormitories, Washburn Hall (1906), named for Duluth attorney Jed L. Washburn, and Torrance Hall (1910), named for Ell Torrance, president of the State Normal School Board, were built.

According to Jacqueline Moran, oral history coordinator for the University of Minnesota Duluth archives, both facilities opened as girls' dorms; Torrance had a dining room.

For more than half a century, Torrance continued to be used as a dormitory, first for Duluth Normal School, then for Duluth State Teachers College, which succeeded the Normal School in 1921, and then the fledgling University of Minnesota Duluth in 1947. Today, Torrance Hall is a privately owned apartment building.

Washburn Hall now serves as home to the University of Minnesota Extension Service-St. Louis County and to the Minnesota Sea Grant program.

"Old Main," the original classroom building of the Normal School, was later utilized by Duluth State Teachers College. In

1947, it provided the first facility for UMD. It was gutted by an arson fire in 1993.

    Old Main, Torrance, Washburn and an adjacent Lab School were placed on the National Register of Historic Places in 1985. The area where Old Main once stood is now a park.

Duluth News Tribune
Then & Now
Feb. 14, 2001

The Twin Ponds on Skyline Parkway are a Duluth landmark. Located on the circular drive that surrounds Enger Tower, the ponds have provided enjoyment for generations.

"Gibson's Duluth 1901," a book lent to the *News Tribune* by Bill Harris, shows an "excursion party (of horses and buggies) on the Boulevard" at the turn of the 19th century, pausing to enjoy the location. The 1901 photograph looks east from the west pond.

Our current photograph also is of the east pond and looks west.

The east pond, closest to Lake Superior, has been regarded as the local swimming hole for decades. The west pond has traditionally been the place to catch fish.

Lorraine McDonald Rawn, 77, who grew up on 21st Avenue West, recalls that she and friends enjoyed long summer days walking, and sometimes biking, up to the Twin Ponds, talking all the while. Rawn learned to swim there and recalls that they dove in with tire inner tubes and had a marvelous time. When their big brothers were around, the girls sat on their shoulders, "playing silly games like trying to knock each other off into the water."

The west pond, toward the golf course, was mostly used for fishing, she said. A rope dangled from a tree branch near the shore of that pond. Rawn said her brother, Bob, used to swing out over the pond, then perform a swan dive to the admiration of bystanders.

The Twin Ponds are fed by Buckingham Creek, which begins in Duluth Heights, east of Observation Road and fairly close to Arlington Avenue. The creek meanders through Enger Golf Course. Tim Howard, project administrator for the city of Duluth Department of Administrative Services, said that the earliest record of deeds shows

that in 1930 there was a work order calling for the "filling of lower lake, Twin Lakes." He noted that they were referred to as Twin Lakes in early documents. That date would have coincided with the Works Progress Administration, established to help Depression-era workers.

The lower pond is drained about once a year in the spring to clean it up, city plumber Steve Shoberg said. The pond above it is natural. He recalls that the pond had "a really nice changing house built about 25 years ago" that had to be torn down several years ago. A bluestone wall, built during the time of the WPA, still stands, however.

Duluth News Tribune
Then & Now
Aug. 8, 2001

Restored once in the 1940s, the Viking ship was rotting by the early 1980s when a Save Our Ship group was formed by local residents. Preservationists raised money to restore the ship.

In the winter of 2000-01, the restored historic attraction was moved to its permanent home in Leif Erikson Park near 12th Avenue East below the Rose Garden. After a vandalism incident in 2001, the city of Duluth gave $34,000 for the engineering and design of a roof structure to protect the ship from the elements. It wasn't enough money and funds are still being raised to finish that project.

About the park: Land purchased circa 1911-12 for a park, extending from Eighth Avenue East to Chester Creek and from London Road to Lake Superior, was at first known as Lakeshore or Lakefront Park. In 1927, Duluth furniture magnates Bert Enger and Emil Olson donated a Norwegian fishing vessel, built to resemble a Viking ship, to the city. Their only condition was that the park be renamed. Leif Erikson Park was dedicated Sept. 8, 1929.

Duluth News Tribune
Then & Now
Jan. 10, 2005

For nearly a century, a wide swath of Duluth — starting at the Point of Rocks and ending near the ore docks — was known as the West End. Today, with a new moniker that honors the area's most lovely natural asset, it is known as the Lincoln Park neighborhood. This file photograph from July 1970 shows businesses on Superior Street, from about 19th to 24th avenues west. West End Liquors was at 1902 W. Superior, Beck's Furniture was at 1904, Duluth National Bank was at 2000 and across the street, the Seaway Hotel

was — and still is — at 2001 W. Superior Street.

Today's view shows redesigned curving streets winding through the Lincoln Park business district, where the US Bank occupies the bank building at the corner of 20th and Superior and many businesses continue to thrive.

Duluth News Tribune
Then & Now
Oct. 13, 2003

These two images reflect views almost a century apart and show the evolution of the bridge over Lester River a block above Superior Street.

The first image loaned to us by the Northeast Minnesota Historical Center depicts the first bridge, a graceful three-tiered design built and paid for by attorney and real estate prospector Samuel F. Snively in the early 1900s. Snively later was elected to public office and held a 16-year tenure as mayor of Duluth from 1921 to 1937, but his interest in parks and scenic areas in Duluth had begun years before.

A masterful fundraiser, he urged and got donations of land

for Seven Bridges Road at Lester River, later turning all the land over to the city.

Snively's wooden bridges were later replaced by the city with bridges of stone, which remain today. Prominent design firms were brought in to create a look that fit into the flow of the land and waters.

The bridge has a timeless quality and highlights Duluth's natural beauty.

Duluth News Tribune
Then & Now
Oct. 24, 2001

The Zelda Theatre, at 311 W. Superior St., showed movies from 1917 through 1928. When photographer H. McKenzie shot this circa 1920, billboards out front advertised "Cecil B. Demille's 'For Better for Worse'" and "Today, Eleanor Field in 'A Maid and a Man.'"

Wrapped around the pillars are ads for Paramount and Artcraft Pictures. Above the door, Zelda's claim to fame — "The Theatre with Good Music" — alludes to its deluxe pipe organ.

Today, the site is occupied by Peterson Anderson Flowers, Inc. Owner-manager Karen L. Anderson, who is no relation to the original owner, notes that in the mid-1980s, when the downtown florist moved to that location, workers discovered the building's history.

About 20 feet above the entryway on Superior Street is the Zelda's old projection room. When it was a theater, the floor sloped down, Anderson said. Later occupants included Zelda Restaurant and Boyce Drug. Anderson said she found old movie posters, newspapers, tickets and the restaurant's liquor license.

Peterson Anderson Flowers had its beginnings in 1948, when Lloyd Peterson and Leona

Anderson, both of Duluth, located their flower business near Lake Avenue. Later, it moved to the Phoenix Building, where Gold's Gym is now. Anderson bought the business in May 1978, later moving it to its present site.

What began as a traditional retail flower shop has evolved into a more complex business that includes gifts and special event and interior design items. "Our tag line is, 'We do the usual and the unusual,'" Anderson said.

In 1998, shortly before Valentine's Day, traditionally one of the busiest times of the year for florists, a fire set in the skywalk on a Sunday night caused smoke and other damage to the company. A cleaning crew was immediately brought in and "we were open for business Monday. We managed to carry on," Anderson said.

The fire forced the business to redo its ceiling, which once again unearthed the old projection booth. As a result, a whole new generation learned about the "lost" Zelda Theatre.

Duluth News Tribune
Then & Now
Dec. 13, 2000

I n 1920, groceries were delivered via hand cart from Brown's Store at 32nd Street and Minnesota Avenue on Park Point. The street was not yet paved, but streetcar tracks, a sidewalk and dirt path fronted the store. Owner Charles Brown ran the store from before 1910 until the 1930s, when he retired. Supplies were delivered to Brown's on flatcars, pulled from behind the streetcar from "uptown" Duluth; this delivery method was settled upon because there was no road to drive on.

The photo was donated to the Northeast Minnesota Historical Center by Mrs. Charles W. Nelson, who lived nearby.

You would hardly know a store had been at 3210 Minnesota Avenue today. After Brown left, the structure had various owners and was a grocery store into the 1970s. Until the mid-1980s, it was a beauty salon. The building stood vacant for several years and eventually was torn down.

Duluth News Tribune
Then & Now
May 3, 2000

A bbett's Drug Store, William A. Abbett, proprietor, at 201 W. Superior St., was a fixture in downtown Duluth at the turn of the century. Look closely and you'll see that Superior Street was lined with bricks — as it is today. Second Avenue West, on the other hand, was a dirt road.

Upstairs in this 1899 shot was Menter & Rosenbloom Co. boasting a sign: "Easy to Buy, Easy to Pay, Just Try and Come Our Way." The company sold men's and women's clothing, including "ladies suits, jackets, skirts, waists (corsets), furs, hats and shoes" for a grand layaway payment of $1 a week.

Up Second Avenue West on the side of the Salvation Army building is a sign for People's Theater. According to James Heffernan's chapter on performing arts in "Duluth, Sketches of the Past," by 1900 the city was a thriving metropolis of 50,000

people with several theaters, some of which were known as opera houses. Duluth was a major stop on the circuits of touring theatrical companies, with top actors of the day.

The site where Abbett's had stood was occupied by Montgomery Ward for more than three decades from 1935 on.

Since the mid-1990s, the northwest corner of that intersection has been occupied by Explorations, a retail store offering developmental toys and games, teacher resource materials and children's books. The owners are Erick and Mary Beth Kjolhaug. Above it, the Duluth Skywalk connects the restaurants and shops of Holiday Center to the west and other businesses to the east.

Duluth News Tribune
Then & Now
Sept. 5, 2001

Marshall-Wells began in Duluth in 1886 as the Chapin & Wells Co., wholesale hardware and grocery firm. Albert Morley Marshall bought controlling interest in 1893 and changed the name to Marshall-Wells Co. The company, which retained warehouses and executive offices on the Duluth waterfront, grew to include 14 wholesale offices throughout the northwestern United States and Canada. At one time, it was the largest wholesaler in the world.

In 1955, Ambrook Industries Inc. of New York bought controlling interest and, three years later (in 1958), Coast-to-Coast stores bought the Duluth division of Marshall-Wells-Kelley-How-Thomson, ending the Duluth firm's operation. The sale affected 400 employees.

Today, Red Lobster Restaurant, at 301 S. Lake Ave., Timberlodge Steakhouse and Hawthorn Suites, both at 325 S. Lake Ave., and Old Chicago Restaurant, at 327 S. Lake Ave., now occupy the building once home to Marshall-Wells Co.

Celebrating its second anniversary this month, Hawthorn Suites specializes in extended stays, features a 24-hour business center, fitness center and indoor pool, and 107 over-sized suites, each with a fully equipped kitchen. The hotel incorporates much of the original Marshall-Wells architecture into its design.

Duluth News Tribune
Then & Now
June 14, 2000

S t. Mary's Medical Center had its beginnings in Duluth's West End in the neighborhood now called Lincoln Park.

In 1888, a small group of Benedictine nuns came to Duluth to take over operation of a building built by monks at 20th Avenue West and Third Street. It was offered to the sisters for use as a hospital. The city of Duluth was still semi-wilderness then, and the hospital looked out on the boreal forest. This building, which would later serve as an orphanage and a home for the elderly, became the first St. Mary's Hospital. According to St. Mary's centennial booklet, those Benedictine nuns nursed

Duluthians through the typhoid epidemics of the 1890s, the Spanish influenza outbreak of 1918-19 and provided emergency care for victims of the Hinckley fire of 1894 and the Moose Lake fire of 1918.

Those events convinced one nun, Mother Scholastica Kerst, to look for a site to build a larger and better hospital. The parents of Mother Scholastica Kerst and her sister, Alexia Kerst, also a Benedictine, purchased two lots at the corner of Fifth Avenue East

and Third Street. After overcoming daunting financial challenges, the cornerstone of the new St. Mary's Hospital was laid Aug. 8, 1897. Six months later, the building was ready for occupancy. Most of the 48 patients housed in the old facility, which was demolished several decades ago, were taken by horse and buggy to the new site. Considered the largest and best-equipped hospital north of the Twin Cities, it included the latest sterilizers, which replaced the gas plates

and tea kettles used in the old hospital.

Today, St. Mary's Medical Center continues to be a leader in health care. In 1997, St. Mary's Medical Center and the Duluth Clinic joined to form an integrated health care system. The St. Mary's/Duluth Clinic Health System employs more than 4,600 people through the region. St. Mary's Medical Center is licensed for 380 beds and 46 bassinets.

According to spokeswoman Mary Trip, SMDC is meeting the challenges associated with health care today by focusing on key areas of change — research, technology, innovation and renovation — in order to provide the region with the highest level of patient care.

Duluth News Tribune
Then & Now
May 23, 2001

The Bradley Building at the southeast corner of Superior Street and Lake Avenue was a landmark in Duluth for 70 years. Our archival photograph, courtesy Northeast Minnesota Historical Center, is from the collection of Kenneth E. Thro.

Designed by Duluth architect Frederick German, the building's first two stories, erected in 1909, were home to various stores and offices. Two new floors were added in 1924. The building was named after Realtor Richard M. Bradley of Bradley Real Estate in Boston.

In the 1930s or 1940s,

when this photo was probably taken, Floan Leveroos Ahlen Co., a men's clothing store, stood at 2 E. Superior St. The Smith Shoe Co. was just east of that at 4 E. Superior St.; Kelley-Duluth Hardware was at 6 E. Superior St.; and White Swan Drug Store was at 8 E. Superior St. Note the streetcar tracks still in place curving from Lake Avenue onto Superior Street.

The large building was demolished in December 1979 to widen Lake Avenue in preparation for Interstate 35's approach and overpass.

At the southeast corner today stands a domed stairway shelter and a sign welcoming visitors to the Lakewalk and Lake Place.

The widening of Lake Avenue changed the look of the area. For many years, Famous Clothing Co. occupied the building at

12 E. Superior St. Upstairs was the Knights of Columbus Hall. In 1987, the Electric Fetus opened at that site. It was primarily a music store but added clothing, jewelry and gifts to its stock of music, which now includes rock, jazz, R&B and blues and a section featuring regional artists. One woman recalled that during her teen years a "hippie" store called the Port of Entry occupied a portion of what is now the Electric Fetus building.

Next door, the aging Strand Theatre was Duluth's only "adult" movie house, showing X-rated films in its waning years. Before that, it was one of Duluth's many downtown theaters showing regular Hollywood fare. The theater building is now gone.

Duluth News Tribune
Then & Now
Nov. 7, 2001

A rainstorm in August 1909 rendered the intersection of Lake Avenue and Superior Street a muddy mess. Members of the "street crew" shoveling mud into mounds on the sides of the streets are dressed in suits, as are the passers-by. Note the Tremont Hotel and its unique architecture just behind the Kaiserhof, up Lake Avenue.

Today's photo, shot at the same intersection, shows Technology Village and cars, streetlights and pavement. But look directly behind the site and you will see the same distinctive windows and skyline of the Tremont Hotel, now the Gardner Apartments, some 90 years later.

Duluth News Tribune
Then & Now
June 23, 1999

Fitzsimmons Warfield Co. Foreign & Domestic Fruits was at 126 W. Michigan St. in 1892. In that day, Michigan Street was a bustling hub of small businesses, with Great Lakes package freight-

ers and rail transportation the primary modes of importing goods.

Charles Fitzsimmons and Andrew A. Warfield bought the space in 1890 and opened shop as Geo. W. Martin & Co. By the following

year, it was listed in the city directory as Martin, Fitzsimmons & Warfield and by 1892-93 it was listed as Fitzsimmons & Warfield, still later as Fitzsimmons-Derrig Co. and Fitzsimmons and Palmer.

The window on the right says: "Wholesale butter, eggs, cheese, poultry." There are watermelons and squash on the boardwalk below the left-hand window and the man with crossed arms. In another 1800s-era photo these words show in the upper windows of the same store: "Butter, eggs, apples, imported and domestic cheese, oranges and lemons, berries and all kinds of vegetables, bananas, foreign and domestic fruits."

Today, that site on Michigan Street is simply the back of a building with one of the shafts of the skywalk system bridging the street.

Duluth News Tribune
Then & Now
Jan. 2, 2001

Built in 1891 for Mathew S. Burrows, the "Burrows Block" at the southwest corner of Third Avenue East and Superior Street housed a clothing store bearing his name. M.S. Burrows & Co. was the "Great Eastern One Price Clothing House for Men, Young Men, Boys and Children" until 1905, when it became Columbia Clothing, which still occupies a part of that site.

Burrows' architect designed a home at 1630 E. First St., which is now a bed-and-breakfast establishment known as the "Mathew S. Burrows 1890 Inn."

His nephew, J. Frank Burrows, continued making and selling clothing in the Lonsdale Building long after the Burrows store closed.

Today, a Fanny Farmer outlet store at 301 W. Superior St. occupies the corner site where Burrows' store stood a century before.

According to Pat Maus of the

Northeast Minnesota Historical Center, a listing for Fanny Farmer in Duluth first shows up in city directories in 1948. There were two stores initially — one at the present location and another at First Avenue West. Both were managed by women.

Established in 1919 on the East Coast, Fanny Farmer Candy Co. was named after Fannie Merit Farmer, the leading authority on cooking in her day. She revolutionized the world of food preparation by introducing precise measurement to cooking.

Since 1991, Fanny Farmer Candy Co. has been owned by Archibald Candy Corp. of Chicago. It is the largest retail confectioner in North America, with approximately 725 stores. Archibald owns Fannie May/Fanny Farmer, Sweet Factory and Laura Secord in Canada.

Duluth News Tribune
Then & Now
Jan. 30, 2002

The intersection of Austin Street and Woodland Avenue was the terminus of the Duluth Street Railway Co. in 1923, when our archival photograph was taken.

Across the avenue, at 4021 Woodland Ave., the building to the left was a grocery store and meat market; the proprietor was Mrs. Lulu Schultze. The building with the white awning was listed in the city directory as Alex Grew Grocery, 4025 Woodland. Streetcar rides were a nickel and Duluth's line extended from one end of the city to

the other.

     Today, Woodland Barbershop is at 4025 Woodland and Nam Lee's Restaurant, at 4023, shares the building. Woodland Poochie Parlor is at 4027 Woodland, facing Calvary Road.

Duluth News Tribune
Then & Now
May 10, 2000

The 21-room brick home of Guilford G. and Caroline Woodward Hartley gave graceful elegance to the corner of 13th Avenue East and Superior Street in the first half of the 20th-century.

And what a playground the Hartley children must have had. Out the door and slightly to the north burbled Chester Creek. From any floor, there were magnificent views of Lake Superior.

Born in 1853 in New Brunswick, Canada, financier and entrepreneur Hartley came to Brainerd as a young man, worked for various loggers, then branched out into business for himself in Minnesota and North Dakota. He was connected with practically every major industry of Duluth during his lifetime, including

ownership of the *News Tribune*. Hartley died in 1922.

In 1954, the Hartley home (included in the estate of Mrs. Walter Congdon, his oldest daughter, who died in 1953) was sold to Gerald Oestreicher & Associates of New York, the firm that owned the Plaza shopping center. The home was torn down to make space for additional Plaza parking.

In January 1992, the site became the new home of Walgreen's, which had previously been in the Plaza across the street.

Duluth News Tribune
Then & Now
Jan. 19, 2000

A wagon, an electric trolley and a vintage car are center-pieces of this street scene at 29th Avenue West and Third Street looking west. The photo, by H.H. Brown, was taken in 1915, when the Jackson Brothers Grocery was at 2902 W. Third St. Next door, at 2904, was the J. August Anderson Drug Store.

Eighty-five years later, the same buildings continue to house

businesses, including Millennium Mortgage and Creations/Pam Dado, a wedding flower shop, at 2902 and Kut-N-Kurl Beauty Salon at 2904 W. Third St.

Duluth News Tribune
Then & Now
March 22, 2000

The unexpected death of Fire Chief Joseph Randall was the occasion for this funeral procession headed east along First Street on June 1, 1927.

A Canadian by birth, Randall, 19, had arrived in Duluth and joined the fire department in December 1886. He became chief in 1909.

At the time of Randall's death, Mayor Samuel Snively was in the middle of his tenure (1921-1936) as four-term mayor of Duluth.

The contemporary shot looks west from Miller-Dwan Medical

Center's outpatient parking ramp.

First Street, which now runs one-way west, is barely visible, but other landmarks — such as the venerable Hotel Duluth, now Greysolon Plaza, and the Aerial Bridge — are in the background.

The original photograph is by two photographers, Blakemore and Oliver, but their first names are not known.

Duluth News Tribune
Then & Now
Feb. 23, 2000

I cicles tell the season of this photograph of homes on Glen Place, likely taken the winter of 1919-20, when the mayor was Clarence R. Magney and the harbor master was William E. Hoy.

Glen Place ran west to east from the north end of Glen Avenue, which ran from Superior Street to the foot of the bluff between 12th and 13th avenues west.

The photograph shows children playing on the board sidewalk between houses marked 1205 and 1207. Each home appears to be a sturdy wooden structure with latticework covering the steep stairways to the front doors.

With the foliage off the trees this winter, the rocks — which once provided a backdrop for these houses — are clearly evident.

Duluth News Tribune
Then & Now
April 12, 2000

The grocery store at 19th Avenue East and Eighth Street — Frances C. Arntson, Grocer — was one of countless neighborhood stores in Duluth. This 1922 photograph shows a streetcar line being installed in front of the business.

Track extensions of the Duluth Street Railway Co. had been completed from East Ninth Street to 13th Avenue East in 1912 and along East Eighth Street to Kent Road by 1923. It was common to see labor gangs of more than 200 men working on track construction.

The 1920-era railway passenger cars were considerably larger than the four-wheel "dinkies" of the previous century. The modern cars, run by motormen, had eight wheels, not to mention windows running the length of each car.

By 1922, electric car "streetcar" service included Piedmont Avenue, Morgan Park, Kenwood, Gary-New Duluth and East Eighth Street all the way to Kent Road.

Eventually, the Arntson grocery became the University IGA Market and, in the late 1960s, Taran's Market, which has served as a neighborhood grocery at various addresses.

Duluth News Tribune
Then & Now
Jan. 26, 2000

Superior Street looking west from Second Avenue East in 1891 was a bustling place with horses and wagons, an electric trolley and awnings over many of the storefronts.

On the lower (lake) side of the street are (from far left clock-wise): City Hall, 132 E. Superior (note pedestrians in front of it); the city jail, 126-128 E. Superior; P.G. Kraemer Co. Flower and Feed store, 120. Across the street (continuing clockwise) is the Pastoret-Stenson block, then the Black and Tobin Meat Market, 123 E. Superior; the Burg-Kugler block, 125-127; and Edward Feibiger Hardware at 129 E. Superior.

Today, Art Options at 132 E. Superior occupies the building that housed City Hall more than a century ago;

Architectural Resources at 126 E. Superior is where the city jail was; Shel-Don Reproductions is at 124; Last Place on Earth occupies 120 E. Superior; Duluth Area Chamber of Commerce at 118; Muffler Clinic, 112; Chinese Dragon, 108; North Shore Taekwondo, 106; Old Town Antiques & Books, 102. Across the street now are various establishments, including the Original Coney Island at 107, a huge parking structure and the Fond-du-Luth Casino at 129 E. Superior.

Duluth News Tribune
Then & Now
Sept. 29, 1999

The view looking across Railroad Street at 26th Avenue West was photographed by Elizabeth C. Halbert on April 30, 1961. Most of the residential West End neighborhood that existed then is just a memory.

Occupants of the homes in the 2600 block facing the street and rail tracks in 1961 included an equipment operator at Globe Elevators, an employee of Garon Knitting Mills and several widows.

Tracks in Duluth were used by several railroad companies at the time, including: Canadian National, Central Vermont, Chicago & North Western, Duluth Missabe and Iron Range, Duluth Winnipeg & Pacific, Great Northern, Minneapolis St. Paul & Sault Ste. Marie, Northern Pacific, Chicago, Milwaukee, St. Paul & Pacific

and Soo Line (which had its freight office at 1002 W. Railroad St.).

In 1961, Duluth had 133 churches; five weekly newspapers plus two English dailies (the *Duluth Herald* and the *Duluth News Tribune*) and a Finnish daily; 44 hotels and motels; three movie theaters, the Granada at 109 E. Superior St., the NorShor at 211 E. Superior St. and the West at 317 N. Central Ave.

At the beginning of that decade, the city's population of 106,884 was at its peak, the highest population ever. By 1970, it had dropped to 100,578.

Looking across the freeway today from Courtland Street on the opposite side, one sees the back of a Motel 6 on Helm Street between 26th and 27th avenues west. The small building in the right side of both photos today houses Tyke's Welding and ABF Freight System Inc., both at 202 S. 26th Ave. W. The old Huron and Railroad streets made way for the I-35 freeway.

Duluth News Tribune
Then & Now
June 21, 2000

The pergola of Cascade Park, now at First Avenue West and Sixth Street, is barely visible today from across Mesaba Avenue. When Cascade Park was created by the City Council in 1888, it consisted of 49 acres of choice hillside land.

According to turn-of-the-20th-century interior and exterior photos, the park boasted a bell tower, a pavilion that featured a waterfall flowing into a picturesque lagoon and terraced landscaping.

Today there's much less area (2¼ acres) and the bell tower has been replaced with a pergola, but Cascade Park is still an enchanting spot within a busy city.

Duluth News Tribune
Then & Now
Sept. 1, 1999

Few areas have been transformed as thoroughly as the area across the street from the Depot in downtown Duluth. In 1963, when this photograph was taken, many establishments faced the venerable train station that served, among others, the Northern Pacific and Great Northern railroads.

The Depot, now called St. Louis County Heritage and Arts Center, is today home to exhibits shown by the Duluth Art Institute, St. Louis County Historical Society, Duluth Children's Museum, Lake Superior Railroad Museum and headquarters of the Duluth Playhouse, Duluth-Superior Symphony Orchestra, the School of

the Minnesota Ballet as well as the administrative home of Arrowhead Chorale and Matinee Musicale.

In 1963, when our "then" photograph was shot, Pal's Corner Tavern was at 501 W. Michigan. Addresses moving west along the street included the rear entrance of the Fifth Avenue Hotel, Al's Grill, Saratoga Barber Shop (513) and rear entrance to the Saratoga Hotel,

the Thomas E. Johnson restaurant, rear entrance of the Clift Hotel, Olund Employment Service and Collections Agency, Union Gospel Mission (519), State Department of Employment Security, rear entrance of the Grace Hotel and Soder's Bar and, toward the end of the block, the Gust W. Seline Restaurant.

By 1968, the entire block had been razed. The city

of Duluth purchased the property the following year with a proposed library in mind.

The new Duluth Public Library, designed by architect Gunnar Birkerts to evoke the look of a Great Lakes freighter, now occupies the entire city block between Michigan and Superior streets and Fifth and Sixth avenues West. It is one of the busiest libraries in the state, with nearly a million items checked out annually and more than 400,000 books, magazines, audiovisual and other material in the collection as well as being a vital resource center.

Duluth News Tribune
Then & Now
Dec. 29, 1999

Three views of Second Avenue West and Superior Street looking east, in different eras.

The photo with horses and carriages and the mule-pulled trolley is from "Duluth Illustrated, 1887." Note the weather vane above the Duluth Clothing House, and the power lines on the street (electricity came to Duluth in 1885, the telephone in 1882).

The evolution of the site of the building marked "Silk" was as follows. It was the original home of Freimuth's in the 1800s, then of the George Gray Co. Later, it became Wahl's Department Store. Today Cosmetology Careers Unlimited and Snyder Super Stop occupy

that approximate area. The photo with the street car, circa 1916, shows that Superior Street boasted a brick pavement and an electric trolley. Note the long skirts on women passers-by and the Central High School tower rising high behind the Superior Street buildings. The Banning block (first building on left), site of D. Buchanan Grocer and Suffel Boot and Shoe Company in 1887, by 1916 housed a dentist, an optician and the Happy Hour Theatre.

Duluth News Tribune
Then & Now
July 14, 1999

"Buy it in the West End. It will cost you less," reads the billboard from this 1923 photograph taken on Grand Avenue looking east from 49th Avenue West.

Down the block on the right side is the Empress Coffee Co. at 4832 Grand Ave. This was a photo for a court exhibit for some sort of an accident — probably related to a streetcar, thus the streetcar operator standing in the center of the road.

In 1923, Samuel Snively was serving the first of his four terms as Duluth mayor and the city's population was about 99,000. Streetcar lines ran from one end of Duluth to the other, and ride

tokens had been in use since shortly after World War I, eliminating the time-consuming process of collecting fares and changing money.

An interesting detail: West Third Street, which begins at Lake Avenue, is called Grand Avenue after 34th Avenue West.

Today's photograph shows Our Savior's Lutheran Church, at 4831 Grand Ave., and across the street at 4832 is the Chromaline Corp., manufacturer of film and emulsion for the screen print industry.

Duluth News Tribune
Then & Now
June 7, 2000

There was no Aerial Lift Bridge in this photograph from Duluth's Central Hillside, circa 1880, looking down onto the dirt road that was Lake Avenue. It's likely those sheds behind the houses are outhouses. There was no modern plumbing. All traffic was by foot or by horse and carriage. The section of town we now call Park Point then was called

"Middletown" and was platted as such. Even then, it was popularly called Park Point. A mere 11 years before this photo was taken, Duluth was described by a young visitor as a rough, noisy pioneer settlement, comprised of "trading post, seaport, railroad construction camp and gambling resort…"

Today's view: This view from Nettleton School overlooks

the old Central High School's 230-foot clock and bell tower (1891). You can see the under-construction Technology Village and the now-developed Canal Park area with hotels, shops, restaurants and the landmark Aerial Lift Bridge, first completed in 1905, with movable platform added in 1929.

Duluth News Tribune
Then & N
Au

Duluth

Anna Roettger of Duluth provided this photo for the book.

Her great-grandfather, Samuel Samuelson, had just unloaded milk at the creamery in downtown Duluth and was returning to his farm on the Samuelson Road. The photo was taken at the corner of First Avenue West and Third Street.

Samuel was born on April 29, 1838, in Motala, Oster Gotland, Sweden, and married Selma Carolina Axell in Sweden on November 8, 1863. He and their eldest two sons came to America in 1881 and built the house on the Samuelson Road. Selma and the remaining family joined them a year later.

Samuel died on October 15, 1918, from burns he sustained in the 1918 Fires that swept through the northeastern Minnesota counties of Carlton, Aitkin, Pine and St. Louis killing 453 people and seriously burning another 85. Selma died at age 75, on August 16, 1919, due to the flu epidemic and burn-related ailments. Their farm was completely destroyed by the fire and never rebuilt.

The 2005 photo shows the Cascade apartment building which now stands at the corner of First Avenue West and Third Street.

argaret Laughlin, OSB, contributed this photo taken in 1897 of three homes on Waverly Avenue. The homes were built by Andrew Gibson near the corner of Arrowhead Road and Woodland Avenue. The area was known then as "Oatmeal Hill."

The current addresses are 1907, 1915, and 1925 Waverly Avenue. All three homes are still occupied.

The 2005 photo shows the view looking up Waverly Avenue of homes built in the late 1800s. One home is visible at 1907 Waverly. The other two to the right are hidden by trees.

Judy Kaiponen contributed this 1986 photo for the book of her children in front of a large dirt pile on Second Avenue East just below Sixth Street. The pile was created during the demolition of four houses and excavation for a parking lot as part of the expansion of Nettleton Elementary School which can be seen in the background.

Judy said her children, Linda, 3, and Brian, 5, not only crossed the unbusy Second Avenue East; they did it in bare feet.

The 2005 photo is a view of the school from the parking lot by the school's gym, at Second Avenue East and Sixth Street.

R uth K. Carlson of Duluth lent us a favorite photograph from her collection. "As a den mother in Cub Scout Pack 31, sponsored by Irving School PTA, I took the photo in front of the West Duluth station of the Northern Pacific Railroad in 1956. The Cub Scouts with lunch bags in hand eagerly await the arrival of the passenger train to ride to the Union Depot at Fifth Avenue West and back." The round trip cost per Cub Scout? Five cents.

The West Duluth station was at 428 N. Central Ave., near the intersection of Central Avenue and Grand Avenue, where a McDonald's restaurant now stands.

Carlson added: "One of the Scouts in the photo is currently a district school superintendent in the Duluth area. Another is an engineer retired from 3M. There's also a Duluth businessman and some other 'success stories.'" One is deceased, according to Carlson, and of that young man she wrote: "I still keep the hankie he gave me, his Den Mother, for Mother's Day."

Duluth News Tribune
Then & Now
July 14, 2003

L ois Helewski, a lifelong resident of Duluth, contributed this photo for the book of the Sherwood Building at 320 W. First St., taken in the 1920s.

W.C. Sherwood and Company was established in 1882 and was involved in real estate, loans and insurance.

Radenbush Pianos occupied a portion of the ground floor. On the second floor were offices. The third floor housed bachelor apartments, and there was a three-room house on the top, home to Edward and Freda Roberts (Helewski's aunt and uncle) who were caretakers of the Sherwood Building at the time of the photo.

Helewski remembers visits as a little girl to her aunt and uncle. From outside the cottage on the roof, she watched the demolition of the St. Louis Hotel and then the building of the Medical Arts Building.

She also watched the telephone operators through the windows of the Melrose Building next door and dreamed of becoming a telephone operator some day.

She retired after a long career with AT&T.

The 2005 photo shows the AT&T building which stands where the Sherwood Building once was on West First Street.

Lifelong Duluth resident and businessman Bill Meierhoff contributed this photo of the Marshall-Wells loading dock in the 1930s.

The Marshall-Wells Hardware Company was established in 1893 when Albert Marshall of Duluth bought the Chapin-Wells Hardware Company, also of Duluth, and gave the new business a new name. It was a wholesale company dealing in hardware, saddlery, paints and mining and railroad supplies.

Marshall-Wells was one of the nation's largest hardware wholesale companies, with branches in Portland, Ore.; Spokane, Wash.; Billings and Great Falls, Mont.; Winnipeg, Manitoba; Edmonton, Alberta; and Vancouver, British Columbia.

The original warehouse building was eight stories tall and matched an identical one just to the west. In 1967, the west building was torn down and the top five floors of the existing building by Marine Iron & Ship Building Company, the second

and current owner of the property. When the two warehouse buildings were built, they were the third largest in the world.

In 1998 the warehouse was renovated into the Hawthorn Suites Hotel.

The 2005 photo is of the swimming pool at the hotel. It occupies the same area as the loading dock. You can see the pillars and triangular footings which have been incorporated into the pool.

Our old photographs portray two early locations of what is now First United Methodist Church.

The first facility was built at Third Avenue West and Second Street in 1869. In 1893, a new church was built back-to-back with the first on the same city block — this one at Third Avenue West and Third Street.

At the 1893 dedication ceremony, the largest collection-plate offering ever heard of locally — some $40,000 — was taken in. The balance of the church debt was raised before the day was over. The new church began completely debt-free.

In 1925, a Community House was built on the site of the original wooden church. "The Meth," as it was called, housed a co-ed recreation program open to all, featuring a gym, wood shop, kitchen, club rooms and offices. Programs included Boy and Girl Scout troops, a nursery, basketball league, various activity clubs and a Golden Age club for seniors.

First United Methodist Church also was one of the first in Duluth to offer child care for toddlers. A *News Tribune* article dated Oct. 28, 1951, reported that parishioners Gladys Pauba and Evelyn Maynard were troubled by the way mothers had to drag their small children after them while on downtown shopping errands. They had noted the children were "always wiggling and uncomfortable." They

felt sorry for the mothers and the children, so the two Community House employees began what they called "the playroom project" as a service to people of all faiths and to all in the community.

In 1966, the congregation moved to its present location at 230 E. Skyline Parkway. The church, which has a congregation of about 700, has come to be known as "the copper-top church" because of the hilltop building's roofing material.

Duluth News Tribune
Then & Now
Oct. 10, 2001

For nearly a century, the Glass Block stores were synonymous with shopping in Duluth. According to Pat Maus at the Northeast Minnesota Historical Center, what eventually became the department store had its beginnings in 1887, when John Panton of Morayshire, Scotland, and Joseph Watson of Belfast, Ireland, rented a 1,500-square-foot space at First Avenue West and Superior Street, calling their business Panton & Watson.

Five years later, a weeklong celebration marked the firm's opening at 128 W. Superior St., this time with 11,500 square feet of space on two floors above street level and two below. Their enterprise used a Martin Cash Carrier cable system that carried sales slips and money from departments to a cashier who made change and sent it back in a wire basket. There were 12 arc lights on each floor and a stock of merchandise valued at $300,000.

In 1896, Watson retired and William White of the L.S. Donaldson Co. of Minneapolis became a partner, forming the Panton & White Co.

Three floors were added in 1902 for a total of six, plus a sub-basement for stock.

The company was purchased by F.A. Patrick in 1911. In 1912, its name officially changed to the Glass Block Store Co. Officers were F.A. Patrick, Joseph Cotton, Richard Sellwood, Bently

Neff and Thomas Reynolds.

During the time that F.A. Patrick owned the store, elegant Greysolon Tearooms were added on the fifth floor. With its oak paneling, fine oil paintings and view of Lake Superior, that floor became a preferred luncheon spot for Duluthians. It closed in 1940 to make room for more selling space.

In August 1944, Mercantile Store Inc. purchased Glass Block. Extensive remodeling was done in the 1950s, 1960s and 1970s as the store continued to modernize.

July 25, 1973, marked the opening of the second Glass

Block store in the Miller Hill Mall, four miles from downtown. Eight years later, the downtown site closed — to the chagrin of downtown boosters.

The site of the downtown Glass Block was demolished in 1981 to make way for a new First Bank-Duluth, which later became the downtown location of US Bank.

John Fedo, Duluth's mayor at the time, was quoted in a Jan. 27, 1981, *Duluth Herald* article as saying he couldn't "underplay

the disappointment" of losing downtown's major department store. Glass Block's closing he said, "necessitates a redoubling of our efforts" to make the downtown viable.

The mall Glass Block was sold and reopened as Younkers in October 1998.

Duluth News Tribune
Then & Now
Dec. 19, 2001

IMAGE CREDITS

All images have been digitally enhanced